The Isle of Lewis Chessman
Simon Currie

op

Published 2013 by
smith/doorstop Books
The Poetry Business
Bank Street Arts
32-40 Bank Street
Sheffield S1 2DS
www.poetrybusiness.co.uk

ISBN 978-1-906613-85-3

British Library Cataloguing-in-Publication Data.
A catalogue record for this book is available from the
British Library.

Typeset by Utter
Printed by printondemand.com
Cover design by Utter
Cover image © Trustees of the British Museum
Author photo: Joe Brownlie CBE

smith|doorstop Books is a member of Inpress,
www.inpressbooks.co.uk. Distributed by Central Books Ltd.,
99 Wallis Road, London E9 5LN.

The Poetry Business is an Arts Council
National Portfolio Organisation

Supported by
**ARTS COUNCIL
ENGLAND**

Contents

i.m.

Wilf Noyce – poet, mountaineer

Jane Wynne – my wife, champion of children's rights

Miracle at Madrid Airport

All brought here, ill-assorted,
different demands, destinations,
we are the wheelchair cases,
left outside Iberia's Información
to wait: no information.

Not dumb but no language in common.
Nor blind but avoiding eye contact,
no camaraderie. Waiting for a name
to be called, oddly-pronounced,
and someone to get wheeled away.

Come down *O Benévola Cariñosa*
Our Lady of the Cripples!
Down here to the concourse
like the Pope with a chopper,
carry us off to a better place.

Blue-drop

For Michael E., Los Picos de Europa, Spain

You crouch, a form of prayer
over some mean flower
others have trod unnoticed.
Face buried in grass,
knees, elbows stained,
you stoop too low for sanity,
a man Gideon would not want,
beside you the Wild Flower Key
or the third Collins guide
worn out in ten years.

This meadow is alight,
blazons of yellow, red, purple.
But you search the quizzical,
plants that disguise
their signature of leaf,
pattern of petal, sepal.
They tease with games of I Spy
that switch to crossword puzzle,
binding grief-sown obsession
with the kindest of tendrils.

Back home, you know a bank,
spurge, sanicle in a green shade,
where in April bluebells glow.
You keep a snapshot,
your son against that blue,
a day no scars on show
yet a man seeded with demons.
For you, who watched him sink,
a place of consolation,
for him, a requiem glade.

Itálica

Itálica, Seville.

Cavafy, this Roman city, all leaden jokes in mosaic,
the thickset amphitheatre for games and gladiators,
is not your Ithaca.Yet once it cast a spell.

Emperors on far campaigns sought the way back here,
dreaming of wine and olives, fish brought up the great river,
dark-haired boys off the street, games behind closed doors.

Hadrian longed to arrive where no barbarian frost
would cut down love or leisure. Today, his Samian ware
lies scattered across the hillside.

But evening, after siesta, on the outskirts of town
a courtyard beckons, fountains play, a chessboard
is waiting, tables are laid.

A young man offers a cigarette.
Upstairs the rooms are shuttered.

Lament for a Genet Cat

Genet, genet, you never learnt
the tenet that touching man
would get you burnt.

Civet, brevet colonel in black and tan,
fiddled, meddled where you did not belong,
sidling after a linnet's nest.

Genet, velvet, tail too long,
ten thousand volts shot through the rest.
Circuit: not a sound

but a spit of fire split the air,
transit down to ground,
genet, laid out there,

only your whiskers frizzled,
sallow, fallow, fading pard.

"Genet, genet!" the linnet whistled,
"You so hard!"

Collioure, La Côte Vermeille

The others absent: you now dust,
our boy and girl gone their ways,
I did not plan this journey back,
the place disconcertingly unchanged.

Would they have recalled the boats,
colours as bright as Matisse, Derain
had seen them? Bobbing on a swell
under the lowering sky.

Back then, we watched French sailors,
clowns in pom-pom caps, striped jerseys.
Today they're frogmen in black wetsuits:
lobsters with machine gun claws.

The vermillion pebbles remain,
marbled like jasper, picked up
as we trod over them to reach sand
in a slop-slop of wavelets.

And we all said how warm it was
after our North Sea cold, a bitter cold
that eased the longer one stayed in,
to re-assert itself further out.

Today, the lone bather:
sea too rough for locals.
Brine on my lips a sacrament
forced on a dying Cathar.

No friendly shore, no lugworm squirls,
no Mum and Dad. No wife, the kids
grown elsewhere. No communal pile
of towels and clothes to run back to.

The Battlements at Lille

For you, my love, Saturday is Migraine Day,
from sleeping in. When you wake, the town of Lille
is stood in half your field of vision: fortification spectra,
coigns of vantage for firing cannon.

The pain begins: a barrage strikes your skull,
as loud as the blast of traffic below the fortress.
Poor Lille: its petticoat of bijoux homes and taverns
are topped by battlements, your speech, sight and reason
hammered under a siege that lasts two days.

The Bay-trees at the Villa Engadi

The bay-trees keep watch, six on either side of the porch,
gossip along their row, vet anyone wanting to enter.
Each trunk is a perfect spiral bearing a sphere of leaves,
leather buffed, stained green, set against cream stucco.
Take some leaves! The trees will let you.
Brighten those northern sills with some mementoes.

Since the fire, black slips down from windows, the roof has gone,
niches emptied of statues, doorway filled with debris.
Newspapers showed the line of trees unscathed.
No manicure restrains: will they grow tall, the fight-back known to Horace?
The villa razed, they could form an avenue, unless chopped down
by squatters for firewood when snow mantles the ruins.

There is always a Villa Engadi, that broken façade an emblem
from Oradour-sur-Glane to Mostar, gardens, fountains intact.
Yet villa, bay-trees exist in the mind: only a mirage,
reverie turned nightmare. Will that comfort you?
To draw on one place not destroyed like the rest,
because it may not be real?

Contemporaries

Lunch at a Swiss hotel with a friend, lawyer and mountaineer in his day.
He twirls the ice in an empty glass, points to a glacier high above our terrace.
There, when a student, he fell down a crevasse. A cousin, climbing with him,
was never found. Two years ago the body turned up. He was called to
identify a boy stopped at twenty, who looked asleep, neat in the clothes
of sepia mementoes.

Imagine a Forest
Title from W.S.Graham

Imagine a forest
bright with flowers,
seen from far off.

Close, these change
to bits of cloth slung
from the branches.

Now, make out they
are women hanged,
their feet dangling.

Stand a moment,
then remount,
pedal away

to normal life,
what goes for that
in time of war.

Edvard Grieg at Troldhaugen

The house is white, window-frames black:
an old snapshot. Inside, photographs
catch an elf frozen in frenzied action.

Piano playing, baton waving, leaping off boats,
past birches, our hero apes a Narcissus of poses,
cavorting in cloaks, hats, white tie, black tie, plus-fours.

One shot repeats: Grieg at his piano,
locking us in. Elsewhere he waltzes
around his friend, the giant Björnson.

The music stops, pictures are shrouded,
black ribbons, tassels, dried flowers.
Nina will tend her mausoleum, thirty years of black.

Outside, the sea laps, a tinkle of miniatures,
the last trump a strangled bleat. Birch leaves,
turned butter yellow, drift on water.

The Goat, Svolväer

For Wilf Noyce who taught me to climb

Climbing the Goat
I have to go five feet down
from one horn to the other,
the town cemetery so far below
its gravestones look like gravel.
Holding us, only the school's climbing rope
we call the dressing-gown cord.

Our combined age is fifty:
not much between three of us.
It's ten years since the war ended
and the German officer scrambled up
to throw himself off, down to the graveyard.
I cling to naked rock.

Myvatn, Iceland

For Valgerdur and Niels

What though their paths were never meant
to cross, as they to every sight
took the two parties they were sent,
the Germans claiming all by right,
the British more ambivalent?
No time for love to strike a light
and yet a few brief hours were spent
at Myvat Lake one starry night,
his bicycle beside her tent.

Let glacial waters roar their might
and Thor bestride the firmament.
Let laval outpours vent their spite,
the earth by fiery chasms rent.
Let warriors wake, renew their fight
in ancient feuds that came and went,
while elves waylay and trolls affright.
For love brooks no impediment:
the bicycle will guard her tent.

Dancing to Happiness

At the conference on sexual disorders
in a gothic castle south of Prague,
after the day's discussions
psychologists straightening out
transvestites dance with their charges,
who loom above them: hair-do's, heels.

Who says they haven't earned it?
But what of later, up to bed,
the dungeon turned conference hall
lurid with conjecture. Still,
spinning along with the glitterball,
tonight it helps the world go round.

After the Snow

It snowed for thirty years.
Ivan Ilyich Ivanovich thought
there would be no end to it.
Wolves took up outside his house,
a reindeer clambered on to its roof,
mistaking it for a crag.

Then, one day, the snow stopped
and the sun began to shine.
He pushed open his front door,
looked across the valley
to where the village was
but found that it had gone.

It seemed the whole world
had been reduced to just
his home, with the meadow
of plum and apple trees.
His dog and hens came out
after him. The cow held back.

Ivan Ilyich Ivanovitch
gave a sigh of relief. Now,
there was only himself to think of.

The Cats of Odessa

weave past man's detritus, round bench, litter-bin, rose-bush,
follow a separate set of pathways.

The Museum of Fine Art, stacked with old oils,
has new still-lifes: asleep on laps of lady attendants.

This Saturday in October, near Cathedral Square
couples jump from cars, men mallet-headed, brides brick-faced.

The parallel world pads on, with rituals all its own,
to find what food it can, or squat in sun, eyes shut.

Figure in a Landscape

Today, at Petra, I saw my wife,
seated facing the Treasury where the Siq broadens.
In blouse and shorts, her olive-green sunhat,
she was taking a breather as I wandered round.
She looked much as she always did,
back to her old self, before the weight loss.
Knowing she'd stay put, I kept on exploring,
but, when I turned again, her place was empty.

Above me, cliffs are reflecting afternoon sun
through a range of reds. The Treasury begins to glow.
A three-way stream of people, with donkeys, camels,
carriages, make their way across the Siq floor.
The site – its traders, drivers, every itinerant
scurrying head down – remains indifferent.

Arun Gandhi Goes to the City

On the journey from his village
he keeps nodding off,
lulled by the rhythm of the train,
despite the excitement
of going to Delhi for interview.

A year qualified, he is after a job
as Senior House Officer
at its premier hospital.
A suit lent by an uncle
is folded in his suitcase
on the rack, with a clean shirt.

At the main city station,
he goes to the changing rooms,
strips off, throws his clothes
to the beggar outside,
and has a shower.
Then he opens the suitcase:
empty, everything stolen.

Still, he gets the job.

Tea at Raffles, Singapore

Walk in! Don't be put off, though in its heyday
riff-raff like us would have been shown the door.
It's no matter shorts and T-shirts if you pay,
nowadays anyone can take the floor.

Go early enough to let you grab some chairs
and spy on pot-bellied men who edge bare-toed,
their wives with bags that shed things unawares:
body language to say we've lost the code.

Look upwards: see the elegance of idling punkahs.
Gaze at teak, marble, gilt, as palm-trees wave,
with sparrows flitting one to another, familiars.
Ask for Singapore Slings to send you brave.

Soon, you can shuffle through, avoiding fights
with shoals of Japanese. The place has form:
you're served by Malaysian men, crisp in whites,
grandsons of those who did for Coward and Maugham.

Ambience, not today's guests, intrigues the voyeur:
the times they shook a Sling as if The Great War
had never happened, The Master, lost in languor,
idly ogling the houseboys stood before.

Some people still insist that was the heyday.
For now, it's sandwiches without a crust
and sweetmeats hid in napkins to sneak away.
Although you're free to eat here till you burst.

Ohanami: 'Look-at-Flowers'

Cherry-blossom time, I attend
a 'Look-at-Flowers' ceremony.
Shunsuke Nishiyama, headmaster
of the school where I teach,
invited me last year. In thanking
him and his wife, I must have been
so polite they have asked me back.

Everyone formal, they smile gold teeth
through the etiquette of introductions,
the offering of food and drink.
The teacher says to me in Japanese
"You! Beautiful English girl,
take care you not meet mad Japanese man
who wants to kill you". We laugh pleasantly.

Next week, the even older Festival
of the Penis takes place south of Tokyo.
Cartoon posters pop up everywhere:
matrons mounted on outsize organs.
Quite seemly: tradition hallows anything.
But I don't plan to go. That day,
I've arranged to meet a Japanese man.

The Revenant

(Hector's Dolphins, Akaroa, NZ)

Focussing on the prow,
everyone shouts, points:
starboard, port, too late.
Cameras clash from cantilevered arms,
like sea-worms searching prey.

Suddenly, two, now four
pint-sized dolphins
chop water into prisms.
The boat stops. Targets
tilt to stare back.

One rising just below us
wears the face of our stillborn child:
the son they had not let us hold,
eyes narrowed, lips parted,
a bubble escaping.

He starts to sink,
pewter shading
to umbral, touched
by the stainless immanence of air
then lost again.

The Easter Island Statues

We stand above the shore, staring out to sea,
the look on our faces: hope, without hope,
we wait resigned for boats that never come.

Ancestors out of time, we can't work our way back.
Eyes fixed in their sockets may look alive,
but inside we're dead, non-starters, grimace in defeat.

The past has fizzled out. Trapped on a lee shore,
we endure without purpose, wondering how we came in,
where we were meant to go, fixed to our plinth by doubt.

Now, the sky has darkened but no portents guide us
toward some sort of future. Abandoned, we keep on
gazing at a seascape no longer ours, unfathomable.

Town Square, Trinidad de Cuba

This square, built over centuries,
is well lit mid-evening: palm trees, church, houses
once the homes of those who owned sugar fields
and slaves. Narrow streets lead up to it, run sideways;
men and women pass by, dark as shadows.

I go back to the square, the light, safer there
but game to everyone. Men offer me cigars,
girls, boys, a meal in a private home,
taxis pulled by horse or man. Saying no
to them all, I'm left with one persistent boy,

polite, a big smile. He says he's fifteen,
shakes my hand, asks my name. I tell him,
mention Bolivár. He says that his is John
then counts to ten in English, a feat
which seems an offer, of what is far from clear.
I shake my head. He's gone.

"Me on the SS Oblivion"

We joined this ship three years ago. Or was it four?
Harry arranged it all, said it was cheaper than care
at home in L.A. We sold up and sailed into our sunset.

Can't ask Harry any more. He's gone. Well, not quite.
Here somewhere, down in a freezer, a few more
like him, with cuts of meat. Ship's company, I guess.

Never missed a thing, my Harry. Won't be taking in much now,
still, nice to have him with us, even freight-class.
And he did see it all the first time round.

Now it's the only world I know. A small one, by your third run,
the places, people on board, familiar. Those who give me jabs
or do my hair and nails. I like routine, the day planned.

Don't know how long I'll last, Lisbon, Colombo, Sydney, Hawaii.
Harry says we've enough not to worry. They'll hold him
till I go too: then unload us both together, next time back in L.A.

The Isle of Lewis Chessman

On his throne, the Norse king looks anxious,
mind a blank, not so much King Lear raving
as my father, withdrawn, two years in the bin,
one moment not knowing me, next, in touch:
"It's my birthday soon. Will I be out for it?"

The eyes focus on nothing, lips compressed
as if he's vexed, or maybe he's mislaid
his dentures. Subdued, he grips a scabbard.
I have seen hands locked that way for hours,
fixed on a chair-back, rattling a door-knob.

On the ward, he ignores all the courtiers
around him, even Sister, masquerading
as the Queen. Stuck here on the board,
no more than puppet, he gets moved on
to suit others. Until checkmated.

They lift him still seated on the throne,
to be shoved one square at a time.
He seems a pawn but, if his spouse were taken,
a real one could become the replacement.
For him, there's no such opportunity.

It used to be thought of as a game:
hands, fresh from fighting blood feuds,
marshalled pieces carved from walrus tusk,
to capture an opponent's carls or castles.
But his mind games are over.

Life at the Edge

The people on St Kilda are represented now
by that row of roofless crofts half-circling round the bay.

Those flickering black-and-white films
tell us a bit, though leave a lot unanswered.

What did they eat, apart from rotten gannets,
cheese wrung from ewes' milk, mussels off the shore.

Could they make their own brew, using oats or barley
from patches grown on walled-off bits of scrub.

Was their music only voices
or had they also pipes and fiddles.

Did they wait for winter storms to end,
before they could put to sea again.

And if they fell out with each other,
how did they cool things off in a place
where everyone knew everyone,
too close, too long, their plaid too interwoven.

Did anyone ever get killed, weighted,
sunk in the sea. And, by common consent,
never mentioned again.
No way of telling: all gone.

Return to Assynt

MacCaig, what brought you to a dark, eyeless wreck,
its people pushed to the edge down more than a century?

It looks like the jawbone of a creature aeons dead,
worn down save a few pegs: the odd incisor or molar.

Seen from Lochinver this dull morning,
Suilven, your favourite, is only a blackened stump.

But the shroud gets pulled to reveal a magic carpet,
what once you called your Book of Kells.

Somehow, you made so vast and wild a thing come down
to a single stonechat, the streak of a kingfisher, a shield of spray.

The Isle of Raasay

Long in the soul to bring you here,
at last our ferry surfs the Sound
to reach the old iron-ore pier,
Dun Caan's conning tower gunmetal in rain.

Mountains on Skye across the bay
brighten a moment, as if chuffed
at our presence. With only days left,
we've made it to Raasay: a promised gift.

Two stone mermaids still guard
the shore, with orbs of blind fish.
We drive on north to Brochel;
you walk up Calum's Road, I wait in drizzle.

Back at Clachan, we climb a brae
to view Macleod's ruined mansion,
torched at the end of renovation.
Soon, we must sail over to Skye.
We won't return.

Homecoming (Raasay)
after Henry Reed's 'The Changeling'

Arriving by sea, a calm of blue,
the hills gleaming beyond,
you anchor by your quay,
the faces of stone mermaids
not raising an eyebrow.

You walk over close-cropped turf
to reach the front of your house,
approach the opening door,
your coat-of-arms above,
and come into your own.

Nurse, housekeeper, cook
have known you all your life,
stand there to greet you,
use your first name: as if
you were not long an exile.

Here are your dogs, your guns
and, across the panelled hall,
just as it was, your bookcase.
Your fiction.

One Man's Hill

On the hill, at Kinlochournhead,
I lost you in thick mist
taking too long to cross a stream,
thought I'd found you,
but transformed into a stag,
minus kilt and plaid.

You turned back,
lowered a crown of antlers,
sniffed the air then made off,
abandoning me
without map or compass.

Years later, I was far away
when I lost you again.
Your hill this time the office
at St Andrews, for company
a loaded shot-gun.
No following you then.

Illegals

Fireweed hitched a lift from North America,
got re-christened rosebay willowherb,
chased Brunel to Cardiff along his railway.

Touch-me-not, Himalayan Balsam,
brought on bales of silk cocoons,
catapulted seeds from river to river.

Today, green alkanet crosses the Channel,
moves north-east along our verges,
blue flowers leaving forget-me-not forgotten.

Leopardsbane outstrips it, leap-frogs Perth
to reach Inverness, with yellow suns
that light the roadside to mark its progress.

Uninvited if harmless. Unlike Giant Hogweed
and Japanese Knotweed, brought here, papers
and passports in order, now notifiable.

Standing Stone, Machrie, Arran

A hand points to the sky, red sandstone, bothy tall,
the top serrated fingers. No script, no language
yet who can say the makers lacked eloquence.

We fail to listen, instead see stone in terms
of what we know: Protestant defiance
or giant orange flipflop to flag up a leisure centre.

Nearby are circles, white granite boulders,
mounds, interlocking rings, more sentinel stones:
a grand design without a guidebook.

But lean against the hand, look up to mountains
blocking out the north, chief among them Beinn Bharrain,
the Sleeping Warrior. Take these for bearings.

The Dandy Brush

The Dandy Brush stays in its drawer.
It longs to brush but no-one now
will use it to smarten up the coats.

The Dandy Brush is crudely made:
rough wooden back, two large nails,
the bristles quite worn down.

The Dandy Brush had held its own
down six generations plus
a diaspora from Whithorn to Leeds.

The Dandy Brush, without a handle,
was never used for beating:
not enough leverage.

Grandpa would call in Scots blether
"Boy, gie us the Dandy! There's a laddie."
So I, not he, could brush his coat.

It did not choose to be an heirloom
of no great value, a thing at risk.
Someone who doesn't know

its provenance may chuck it on the fire.
The Dandy Brush wants to see action:
those long black coats again.

The Queensferry Burry Man

Burry Man these past few years
doun at the Ferry Fair. Fer days
they bring the burs tae dry,
cast oot the creepy-crawlies,
then hook burs ontae cloots.

Day itsel', six in the mornin',
lassies stick their cloots
aa' ower me bar hand an fit,
wi' slits tae see an ane fer a straw.
Ma crotch Ah dae masel'.

At back o'nine Ah leave Toon Hall,
start alang the High Street,
stave o' floo'ers in aither fist,
twa lads tae hold an guide me,
gie whisky thro' the straw.

Ah'm daft daein' this agin,
wi' hair sark o' burs.
Nae herrin' left tae raise.
Sae, daein' awa' wi' the deil?
Or gettin' lassies laid
tae carry bairns ower winter.

Gae on, lads, fair stymied.
Canny tho', dinnae stumble.
Nae drink, ma bladder's stoond,
an burs thae're jaggin' me.
Ah weel! Back at Toon Hall fer six
Ah'll strip 'em off an hae a slash.

"How runs the stream?"

I think of the streams I used to fish.
Meanwood Beck had one-trout pools
where catch-and-return was the order.
There I once saw a cock redstart,
perched on a stump in all his finery.

The Nidd at Darley was so overgrown
it held few pools that I could fish,
my lack of skill thwarting me.
I watched, in awe, as upstream dry fly anglers
cast under the lowest of hazel tracery.

But the Ure at Tanfield was broad
and over-stocked, its banks profligate too
with self-seeded soft fruit, Martagon Lily.
These streams no doubt still run,
but not for me, except in memory.

A Fishing Rod

    is enabling:
once I arrived to fish Sour Dub without one.

A fishing rod is a nuisance while travelling:
that land and air trip to Shetland. Never again.

A fishing rod has no other uses than fishing,
apart from poking at moths on a ceiling.

A fishing rod is not a cane for beating a child:
look at Grandpa, who broke his best one.

Flooded Out

First sign of the pest is curious gear
littering the porch. Watch out before
it can breach your inner dam. Never
allow space to a fisherman, whether
as lover or lodger.

His keepnet folded in the hall extends
six feet when a heel gets caught in it.
Weights skitter round washing machines.
Bags of feed spill to clutter doorways.
Maggots turn to flies.

Even what is yours will get pulled in,
lunch boxes punctured to aerate worms,
scissors and camping stools purloined,
socks holed, outdoor clothes patterned
with silver sequins.

Rivers, becks converge from all sides,
bidding to cascade through your rooms.
Dace, chub, roach flap on the carpets.
Whiskery barbel with dead men's faces
loom from mirrors.

Skull and Crossbones

On flagstones here at Cartmel Priory
the icon is repeated, nave to aisle,
below it carved an empty hour-glass.

Crusaders were buried where they fell,
only the skull and thigh bones excised,
made clean, the head salted, wrapped in cloth.

Were widows shown such relics,
lips that had touched their own,
thighs that had lain with them?

Today, past streets and churches flagged,
whole corpses make the journey home.

A lot going on

We're here to survey
the two remaining fields in this village.
They harbour medieval structures.

From walnut trees a posse of rooks
rides away, green nuts in black beaks:
too great a distraction.

Further up, a fresh diversion:
"There's a lot going on in this field,"
says our landscape historian.

He's right: a ram, methodical,
is trying to mount each ewe in turn
but falling off.

Well, nr Masham, N.Yorks

Bone-white

The snow almost gone but enough persists
in troughs and hollows to remind us
we live in a medieval landscape.

Rigg and furrow alternate green and white
down one steep field. In another, the slope
is terraced by snow-laden lynchets.

It brings back the men and oxen
that shaped these half a millennium ago:
a skeletal rap against our door.

Trial by Water

At Fountains Abbey in medieval times
a miscreant or heretic would be put
in a sack, with a piglet and cockerel,
thrown over the bridge into the River Skell.

Should the man escape, he was innocent.
If he drowned, it gave a swift descent to Hell.
The fate of his companions got no mention:
base creatures do not have a soul.

The river must have been deeper then.
It could be that, by inversion,
from Skell to Hell became Helter-Skelter.
Believe that and you'll believe anything.

Roll-call for Old England

"What luckless apple did we taste...!"
– Andrew Marvell

They stand in line, the numbers falling,
to step forward one a day,
the grand, Lady Henniker and Lady Sudeley,
the homespun, Tom Putt, Jester,
Pippin, Annie Elizabeth, Maltster.

Between, come fixers and keepers,
the middlemen: Hawthornden, Ingestrie,
Jupiter Alderman, Grenadier.

These French interlopers
are here as high-ranking brides
or could they be Huguenots?
Orléans Reinette, Calville Blanc d'Hiver
followed by Violette de Montbéliard,

they have in attendance
La Mère de Menage, La Belle de Boskop
from the Court Pendu Plat.

Germans are taking over our Royalty:
Blenheim, Holstein, Gravenstein,
Prince Albert, the Duchess of Oldenberg.

They make slow, stately progress
through Southern Counties: Ashstead,
Crawley, Dumelow, Laxton, St Edmund's.

Flying ahead to warn of their advance
goes the Ildrod Pigeon.

Lady Jane Grey

What are jewels, brocades to me?
No Holbein now to paint them,
gilding the King we feared.
Only Warwick exhibits me,
his last move making me Queen.
Taken in turn by Cousin Mary's bishop,
they leave me not even a pawn.

Two centuries from now, in France
the painter Delaroche recycles me,
a Protestant, for Catholics.
Shows me at sixteen, composed,
clear-eyed before my execution.
They gaze at me, doomed as well,
then clamber on the tumbrel.

After him comes Horsley, who paints me
sanitized, a symbol of purity:
I that am married and deflowered
while still a child. He covers me
save for hands and face:
demure, I seem without a care,
bent over the needlework I detest.

Boundary Names

Fields on a township boundary
were often the poorest land,
hardly worth the cart-ride:
Bare Arse, Empty Purse, Starvation.

Good only for lawless deeds:
Gallows, Dead Man's Rand,
or low yields at lazy margins:
Shameful, Skinny Flint, Spoilt Rein.

Fields as far from the village
as most men could imagine,
stumble on, or scarcely reach:
Botany Bay, Come by Chance, World's End.

But look for them on old maps
to find lost lanes and townships,
land disputed then abandoned:
Cain's Piece, Poverty, Poor Gains.

Once, rival townships went on
joint perambulations, wrangling
over scraps or *knoblits* of ground:
Stony Tang, Scrape Bone, The Scraggs.

At Gardham Lock

For Peter Didsbury

Canals bring back a past we never had:
transport that knew to take its time,
those low-browed cottages where sad
women waited for husbands to come home,
their pallid daughters coughing from the damp
to end in churchyards long before their mothers
or disappear in water till the thump
of a keel turned them up to face their brothers.

Now, places of birdsong, reeds and rushes,
with English flag as memory's fleur-de-lys,
a yellow phoenix springing from the ashes
of humdrum lives we can no longer see:
be-whiskered men, their horses on the towpath,
half-laden barges idling from wharf to wharf.

Pocklington Canal, Melbourne, East Riding

The Griffins at Wallington

These chimeras were brought
from Bishopsgate for ballast:
an empty collier sailing back
London to Newcastle.

Ozymandias in a northern park,
four heads rest on sober grass
as if, landlocked icebergs,
their bodies bulked below.

No more than emblems,
they face rude frosts,
gaze from blank orbs
that give away nothing.

So odd, they make strangers seem
familiar, greeted but come back
from more than fifty years ago
to stare them out.

Beckett's Park, Headingley

The oaks and Spanish chestnuts
of this suburban lung
are said to have been planted
in the battle formations
of opposing armies at Waterloo.

The specimens look old enough.
But you'd need an air balloon,
map of the battlefield
and a good sense of 3-D
to work things out.

And over the years
some will have been lost:
to storms, rotten forks,
flowerbeds, wartime allotments,
not cut down in ranks like men.

"Kismet, Hardy. Kismet"

That's what he said, they told me later.
He was being philosophical:
Fate, Life and Death sort of thing.

I'd misheard him. Thought it a bit odd
as he was never one for the midshipmen.
Still, with Emma not around

I did my best, held him in a half-Nelson
(in truth, what was left of him),
gave him a smacker he wouldn't forget in a hurry.

In return, he gave me the eye:
I can see the look on his face even now.
But then, he died: Kismet!

A Bleak Text

Seat, domain, citadel:
a Victorian's place in the world.
Samuel Irton, of Irton, Cumberland,
last of the Irtons, dead,
eight hundred years at an end.

Their dark brown church
remembers three sons,
fixed in marble relief,
enough, it must have felt,
to make Irton safe.

One left broken
by Indian Army Service,
others lived long enough
to praise in stone their mother's
knowledge of scripture.

In turn, Samuel's widow,
her estate on earth empty,
chose from Hebrews XIII:14
a text without comfort:
"Here we have no continuing city".

Orde Wingate of the Chindits

His name had a plaque to itself in the Memorial Chapel.
A loner, we took him as a hero but somehow
not quite right: no regular British Officer.

He bucked authority, didn't play the game.
If he had been old enough for World War I,
he'd have gone behind enemy lines,
not leading charges from the front.

In the Burmese jungle he fought dirty,
crawled through swamps and streams
to stab sentries in the back or throttle them with lianas,
throw grenades to overrun gun-posts.

After such derring-do, his death in a plane crash
was no Boys' Own action. It left us feeling
he'd missed out, deserved another go.

A Tide-rip Taking Language

The man who mapped the dialects of England came in under my
care after suffering a stroke. He told me things I'd never heard
before, like the wealth of names for the common newt. These ran
from *ask* to *watter-eff* through variants such as *eft*, *eut* and *evet*.

He said that such a mix of words was common in countryside
long impoverished, where richness of language would persist.
Folk who sailed to America, escaping drudgery or persecution,
brought their pet names for things they found as settlers.

Aware he would not get home, all we could do was talk. But,
when he died, his raft of knowledge dimmed to publications.
Newts were declining, the names for them fallen into disuse.
It felt as if a burial ship of words had been ripped out to sea.

RS Thomas at Aberdaron

Man of stone, drab as wet slate
inscribed with dark ideas,
you stand in this your place of work,
gaze out at sea patterned by windows,
ignore the scatter of people
knelt before you.

Do you care about these sinners
or must their travail stir you to write:
striving with cattle mired in lanes,
grappling boats on a lee shore?
Hardships of men today and others
long entombed.

You summon brimstone,
calling for English second homes
to be torched. Yet you'll also
heighten language, tighten rhythm
to conjure up the blaze of light
on a small field.

Nobody's Hero

i.m. Wing Commander Jimmy Romanis

Eighty five, his life become a cock-up,
Jimmy can't cope with "Battleship".
He loses two destroyers, his aircraft carrier,
but then starts to talk about the real War.
We give up playing, settle down to listen.

"I taught them how to fly Hudsons.
RAF Silloth, Cumberland. Only mountains to miss.
Had to be landed nose down, that plane,
dead against regulations, or the engines
might tear off in a ball of fire.

One time I did it, the visiting top brass
was so angry, he stormed from the cockpit,
strode off without another word
to his staff car. Marked me down
as not fit for promotion.

Later, I flew bombers, Hamburg, Dresden, Berlin.
Often in daylight, for pinpoint bombing,
so low we could see people staring up.
Once, I limped home over the North Sea,
behind me Joe, my navigator, dying."

By the end of the War,
Jimmy had taken flak
from both Higher Command in England
and anti-aircraft guns in Germany.

Sixty years on, he makes it sound a game.

Maple

Field Maple Acer campestre

On the way down to the river,
I push aside exploding balsam
to meet my childhood self
on the way up with a five-point leaf,
pillar-box red, found
floating in dappled water
below the maple tree.

Pressed in the back of our Bible,
it fades as dull as any leaf.
But the tree can shed and renew.
In autumn, its leaves turn red again,
red as the belly of the stickleback
in a jar safe on the loop of string
I hold in my other hand.

Llewellyn

They said he was quite somebody
before the War: 'Mr Borneo Timber'.
But that was before the Japanese,
the Burma Railway.

When I was eight I heard them say
he came home weighing six stones
and all his skin tore off like tissue paper.
"How did he get it back on?" I asked
but they changed the conversation.

Then, at a family lunch
he was next to me, his shirt-sleeves rolled up.
I studied the arm that held a fork.
It looked normal to me.

"Is it yours, Uncle?" I whispered,
stroking the hair on his forearm.
"Hey!" they shouted, "That's enough.
You keep your hands to yourself!"

But maybe those hairy bits
weren't his at all.
Like Jacob pretending he was Esau.
As for his mind, they said that was gone for good.
And soon he stopped coming round.

Dust

Not so much cliff as mud-slide:
sixty years on, our hut (sleeps five)
floats somewhere in the air
above the beach. Gone too
the lawn, the fence with roses,
the steps that climbed to these.

Dad tended those steps alone
though we would scatter sand
in running up from a swim,
shivering as we waited
to be wrapped in towels.

I see them now, our parents,
leaning over the gate
to greet folk here for the day.
All of them turned to dust,
they leave only tongues of mud
coming down to our beach.

The Lake Hotel

We have come down to the far end
of the garden, the part beside the lake.
But this is more than fifty years ago.
The ghosts of my parents, who stayed
here visiting me, have not lingered.

I imagine us all, on this bench,
now rotten, as they try to get from me
whether or not I am guilty as accused.
To let them face up to School
or take me away in disgrace.

Dad's Secretary

She should have been a singer.
When she did *Just a Song at Twilight*
on the promenade above the sea,
the audience went quiet,
even the waves checked a moment.

Her husband was accountant
to a chain of butchers.
She brought us long pork pies
with an egg up the middle.
Dad always got the yolk.

Her grandpa had ships in Liverpool.
She told us he looked like the figure
on the Quaker Oats packet,
holding up a mirror that showed him
with another mirror then another and so on.

I wondered how that voice would echo
down the hall of mirrors at Temple Newsam.
And whether getting the egg into the pie
was like putting a ship in a bottle.
And if, with a big enough magnifying glass,
I would see her grandpa get smaller
and smaller, down to the last iota.

When Half the Map was Red

Great-Uncle Alexander, the Governor-General,
wore a hat peaked at both ends,
the shape of an upside-down ship,
with braid along the gunwhale
and tassels fore and aft,
the figurehead on the prow
either a flattened mermaid
or Queen Victoria.

When he acted as her stand-in
people approached him on a dais.
The hat would tilt up and down,
its tassels like Goldenrod in a breeze.

Later, back in Blighty,
we hid in the spare room
to lift the hat from its box,
silk-lined with a crested label
and yellowing paper.
When I wore it, my head
went right inside. I became
some new invisible exotic creature.

RAF Blue

Did they dress to cadge a lift? Or was it regulations?
Thumbing us at the roadside, stiff in their light blue serge.

People said they had warrants, did it to graft money,
you might get mugged and, anyway, trains were good.

The same age, through my test so driving alone, I viewed them
with curiosity but unease. Never picked one up

yet felt guilty about it. Thought of the moment
he would turn to smile when I dropped him off,

my hand on the rough warm blue of a perfect crease,
engine left idling. Until he made to get out.

On Not Wanting to Do Medicine
River Greta, Ingleton, 1957

Escaping from caves and pot-holes
one frosty January morning,
this boy, eighteen, climbs along
the banks of a river: its waterfalls
turned icicles that tease the sun.

Here, he meets tame squirrels
as red-haired as he is, eager to share
his lunch and throw off winter.

He's not dragooned down Gaping Gill
another day, its charnel-house smell,
tunnels spot-lit: a night ward
where someone is dying, the glare
from the carbide lamp on his head.

Just him, the sun and squirrels,
redheads all: to do as they please,
for a few hours, at least.

Anatomy

To dissect 'Head and Neck',
Rupert chanced to get the body
of his old flute teacher.
He took delight in studying
if the muscles used for blowing
were over-developed.

I hoped that somebody
might one day get the chance
to dissect Rupert's brain,
an organ lacking a sense of proportion,
the lobe for propriety missing?

Altruism

This, they told us at Mill Hill,
was cutting-edge neurophysiology.
We stood and watched in silence
as cats, one a tabby like mine at home,
miaowed, yawned, looked back at us
while pinned down, wired up,
crowned by gadgets in their brains.

Dr Wilhelm F.,CBE,
the chief vivisectionist,
spoke to us in broken English,
while pressing knobs which made
a paw lift, a face scowl, a tail twitch.
His actions stoked our xenophobia
in those incorrect fifties.

My tutor bade me welcome research
that helped us understand
how our own bodies worked.
But, years later, I was glad
to see the good doctor
given a long suspended sentence
for cruelty to animals.

Some Picnic

High summer, the corn high,
cycling downhill towards a bend
I see more than from the car.
Over the hedge, a rectangle,
darker green than the rest.
I halt, weight on one leg,
look beyond where hawthorn
has parted, to close again.

A car, the top of a car,
I mark it clearly now,
no crop circle.
And there is the driver,
seated low in the corn,
facing towards his car,
into the sun. He grins at me.
Odd place for a picnic.

Two days later, nearby,
I make the detour,
climb up to the bend,
find the car still there.
So too is the man,
eyes closed now
but the grin broader,
lips drawn, teeth bared.

Not Covered

I stand in the hall
with the young man
here to mend the Hoover
kneeling before me.
He has a fine head.
We are alone in the house.

The second time in a year
we've needed him,
covered by warranty.
I forgot he looked like this.
I could almost touch the soft fair
hair on his neck.

The Pot of Roses

This time of year, across
the living room, sunlight falls
on Barlow's still life in oil:
roses in an earthenware pot.

Oils lap up such light,
watercolours must shun it.
The roses glow, fair ready
to burst out of the canvas.

Did the artist have any idea,
when he was painting them,
they were capable of this?
Springing to life on their own?

Think how those sombre scenes,
oils hung in halls and kirks,
their varnish darkened, might look,
brought out to reap the sunshine.

At Stonegrave

the works of art left me dumb,
except for a stone with a hole in it.
"This one! You find them on the beach."
"Ah!" his widow corrected me, "You mean
the *objet trouvé* Magritte brought from the Nord."

After that, everything the kids found
was an *objet trouvé*. Martin, aged three,
would bring a bucket of treasures home
and arrange them on his duvet.
But would Magritte have kept that dog poo?

"Und hier, Doktor"

After the war, we saw Poles,
moustaches drooping at the corners,
hair thin if still fair, grey kept for eyes.

They gave no history but, once on the couch,
would point everywhere:
the pain *"ist hier und hier und hier"*.

Nothing to find, nothing to do for them,
they soon dressed again and shuffled off
resigned, without a word.

Sometimes, one got angry,
might lunge across the desk,
but, when restrained, went docile like the rest.

At Dom Polski, Chapeltown, we ate hot beetroot
with the Prime Minister-in-Exile,
his bearing upright, moustache stiff.

A butcher's boy

from up the coast
has taken over the shop in our village.
Handsome but brawny, more bullock than Adonis,
he must spend evenings carving chunks off himself
that grow back overnight.

Sunday will give respite and early closing Wednesdays.
But, now it's my turn, I feel squeamish.
Think what to avoid: "Have you any spare ribs?"
or "I'd like some of your tenderloin"
a bit near the bone.

His 'phone rings. I motion him to answer, overhear
he's soon to wed. So sweetbreads are off.
Will it get halted, the girl put her hoof down?
Or might things escalate: veal, with baby onions?
"Your bacon's good." He blushes.
But liver's gone: that eagle.

Bridegroom

That first night, the Grand at Scarborough,
they got to their room, tired but happy,
to find the walls a gallery of wings.

He knew at once: dead rooks
nailed all over the shop.
Two of his shooting pals
had nipped out from the reception,
climbed up a handy drainpipe,
got in through an open window.

His wife of a few hours had hysterics.
The first time he'd seen her go like that!
They gave her another room, of course.

The Lower Jaw Trick

That move, accomplished only once,
when, comfortably seated, shot-gun cocked,
cartridge loaded, muzzle in your mouth,
you pull the trigger with a big toe (either will do).
People who know about such things tell me
it takes off all your head above the lower jaw.

The sound brings anyone in earshot
to find a colourful scene:
blood and brains up the wall,
you, sat on your chair insensate,
natty moustache gone forever,
that smile wiped off your face.

The nearest I have got to such a sight
is when my mother made me visit an aunt
whose pressure cooker had blown up,
a grain of barley stuck in the safety valve.
Walls and ceiling were draped in fronds of leek,
a pattern William Morris would have died for.

Drive Dog

"The dog's stripped its teeth."
He looks relieved: a small job.
"The dog?" I ask. He beams,
taking me for would-be mechanic.
"Up here they call it the bush
but where I'm from it's the drive dog."

"And teeth?" "Yeah," he grins,
showing his own canines,
"Four teeth. It's part of the..."
but he's losing me, knows it.

"Anyway, no need for a new dog,
I've packed yours with acrylic.
Hardens within an hour.
Then you can turn things on
and it'll run like a greyhound."

No having to put the dog down.
Or a dental plate made.
And I can take my donkey jacket off.

A Leaving Do

We realised he would go unnoticed
so threw together an assortment of nibbles
and people he might have got on with,
set in the library at lunchtime
to furnish some sort of farewell.

Nobody could think of much to say
but we kept on smiling at him,
drank some cheap white wine
out of plastic cups to wish him well
and then got back to our work.

Bumping into him years on, I said
"I thought you'd gone to Dorset."
"No, that was our son, the dentist.
Audrey and I never left.
We've been here all the time."

Archaeopteryx

This fall on compacted ice
finds me spread-eagled,
arms that may be wings
pinioned across the road,
the pattern of knitted gloves,
one stuck at each wing-tip,
impressed as primitive feathers:
a sudden extinction.

Not being Archaeopteryx,
I can pick myself up,
step bird-like to safety
of thistle fused with grass
and snow along the verge,
to leave behind a conundrum,
etched on unyielding ice
that does not mean to melt.

Notes on Contributors

Shade Precious, poet, writer, critic,
Shane P------, twelve, lively, affectionate,
is published in many prestigious magazines.
has had many foster-homes.
He has a collection "The Coming Man"
He is a boy with a mild learning difficulty,
looking for a publisher "who cares for my oeuvre".
looking for parents who will care about him.
Shade has a pad near Oxford
Shane has never had a home
with a dog and two wives,
but is very fond of animals
called Errata and Pro rata,
and would like a dog or a cat
plus a stray cat known
to call his own.
as the Wandering Muse, the name
Please use the name in this journal
of the journal he edits.
to contact Shane and us.

Patron Saint of Pianos

Blessèd is Miles Coope,
five foot four and dead at fifty-four,
Miles, who lifted my piano up two flights
with help from just one lad
and none from me.

That Steinway upright he and I bought
from a lady in Baildon, whom Miles
beat down further than I would dare.
He told me grands were easier on stairs
because they came apart.

Miles, who once charged a pittance
for a day spent cleaning one up
at Batley Variety
after Lulu's accompanist
had knocked over a tray of lagers.

Heaven, like Imperial France,
sidelined its pianos for harps.
So Miles can do his chords and scales,
cosseting keyboards for their own sake,
and leave all tunes to the Devil.

Visitor

Death arrived yesterday:
no knock on the door,
just showed up in the hall.
Polite, self-effacing,
wanting to be no trouble.

Turned down a cup of tea
but took a chair,
carried it to the landing.
From there, he could watch
our bed, though not to pry.

Rather, he sat, cowl hiding
his face, hands clasped
like a set of ivories.
The cat upstairs went
the long way to her bowl.

Tonight, he may still be there
if both of us are too.

On Reading Barker's "Summer Song"

Wykeham Arms, Winchester

George, how did you contrive
to realize such tenderness?
You, who would break in
a woman then bunk off,
leaving a trail of kids
and unpaid bills?

My companion for dinner,
your flourishes on the page
blot out the babble
from nearby tables.
You, a bringer of woe,
help me to weather it.

A summer ago, in this city,
the laws of chance implied
true love went on for ever.
Now, even ducks on the river
live in hope, while I endure
your "everywhere of grief".

Finding Caerhun

Why go back to where times were happy,
when doing so disturbs as much as comforts?
Better to visit places that kept their heads down,
letting one pass them by until today.

So to Caerhun, left alone in a field
up river from Conwy, Roman fort on a bluff.
One corner guards a chapel now the church,
fed by a track that dies on reaching it.

Monks robbed sandstone for lintels, pillars,
their building almost as old as the fort itself.
Geese patrol mudflats below soldiers' bath-houses.
The main road, across the river, serves a few farms.

Here there is no-one but me, walking over the square
that makes the fort, its banks cut by the lane.
Somewhere to start afresh, no sad associations:
graves with columbines and poppies not my concern.

Orchids

Orchids are opportunists,
springing up in crevices
or next to cowpats.

They know how to tease:
one in the west of Ireland,
marsh or butterfly, stays
in bud, the flower-head
set to reveal itself
only once we have left.

Orchids are promiscuous,
a host of hybrids fathered
to confuse further.

But they are generous too.
Back home, a sloping field
above a stream, with clapper
bridge and fallen ash-tree,
is filled, white to blood-red.

My wife and I came here.
The next June, I brought the kids
three days after she died.

This time, a lone pilgrimage.
Orchids keep their side of the bargain.
Year after year they come back,
whether or not we can.